Milly, Mo

and the Pumpkin Seeds

"We may look different but we feel the same."

It was market day.

Milly and Molly found an old radio they couldn't leave behind.

They carried it home, dusted it off

and turned it on. Milly and Molly held their breath.

"Parts of Africa are gripped by famine," said the newsreader. Then the old radio died with a crackle and a pop.

Milly and Molly were aghast. What could they do to help?

They decided to share the distressing snippet of news with Farmer Hegarty.

Milly and Molly found him contemplating a thousand little pumpkin plants that had popped up in the place where he fed his pigs.

"Look at this," he said. "Give a pig a pumpkin and out the other end will come a pumpkin seed in a dollop of manure, all set to grow in the spring."

It was Milly and Molly's turn to contemplate.
They had an idea.

"Farmer Hegarty," they asked. "If we give a bird a pumpkin seed, will it come out the other end in a dollop of manure, all set to grow in the spring?"

"I don't see why not," said Farmer Hegarty. "How do you think I get little blackberry plants popping up under my trees?"

"Farmer Hegarty," they asked again. "Could a migrating bird carry a pumpkin seed to Africa?"

"It's worth a try," said Farmer Hegarty.
"What a great idea!"

Milly and Molly knew all about migrating birds. They loved to lie in the grass and watch the swallows fly away to warmer countries in the autumn.

Milly and Molly spoke to the swallows.
Their idea was taking shape.

In the summer Farmer Hegarty helped them gather a thousand pumpkin seeds.

In the autumn the swallows each took a pumpkin seed as planned.

They circled their goodbyes before they flew off on their long journey to Africa.

Over the winter Farmer Hegarty took the old radio apart and put it back together.

Milly and Molly turned it on. Had their idea of growing pumpkin seeds in Africa worked?

The old radio crackled. Milly and Molly held their breath.

"A miracle has happened," said the newsreader. "There are pumpkins for Africa!"